Tattoo

Placement

Theme

Planned Date

Palette

Placement

AF118823

Design

Detail 1

Detail 2

Notes

Tattoo

Placement

Theme

Planned Date

Palette

Placement

Design

Detail 1

Detail 2

Notes

Tattoo

Placement

Theme

Planned Date

Palette

Placement

Design

Detail 1

Detail 2

Notes

Tattoo

Placement

Theme

Planned Date

Palette

Placement

Design

Detail 1

Detail 2

Notes

Tattoo

Placement

Theme

Planned Date

Palette

Placement

Design

Detail 1

Detail 2

Notes

Tattoo

Placement

Theme

Planned Date

Palette

Placement

Design

Detail 1

Detail 2

Notes

Tattoo

Placement

Theme

Planned Date

Palette

Placement

Design

Detail 1

Detail 2

Notes

Tattoo

Placement

Theme

Planned Date

Palette

Placement

Design

Detail 1

Detail 2

Notes

Tattoo

Placement

Theme

Planned Date

Palette

Placement

Design

Detail 1

Detail 2

Notes

Tattoo

Placement

Theme

Planned Date

Palette

Placement

Design

Detail 1

Detail 2

Notes

Tattoo

Placement

Theme

Planned Date

Palette

Placement

Design

Detail 1

Detail 2

Notes

Tattoo

Placement

Theme

Planned Date

Palette

Placement

Design

Detail 1

Detail 2

Notes

Tattoo

Placement

Theme

Planned Date

Palette

Placement

Design

Detail 1

Detail 2

Notes

Tattoo

Placement

Theme

Planned Date

Palette

Placement

Design

Detail 1

Detail 2

Notes

Tattoo

Placement

Theme

Planned Date

Palette

Placement

Design

Detail 1

Detail 2

Notes

Tattoo

Placement

Theme

Planned Date

Placement

Palette

Design

Detail 1

Detail 2

Notes

Tattoo

Placement

Theme

Planned Date

Palette

Placement

Design

Detail 1

Detail 2

Notes

Tattoo

Placement

Theme

Planned Date

Palette

Placement

Design

Detail 1

Detail 2

Notes

Tattoo

Placement

Theme

Planned Date

Palette

Placement

Design

Detail 1

Detail 2

Notes

Tattoo

Placement

Theme

Planned Date

Palette

Placement

Design

Detail 1

Detail 2

Notes

Tattoo

Placement

Theme

Planned Date

Palette

Placement

Design

Detail 1

Detail 2

Notes

Tattoo

Placement

Theme

Planned Date

Palette

Placement

Design

Detail 1

Detail 2

Notes

Tattoo

Placement

Theme

Planned Date

Palette

Placement

Design

Detail 1

Detail 2

Notes

Tattoo

Placement

Theme

Planned Date

Palette

Placement

Design

Detail 1

Detail 2

Notes

Tattoo

Placement

Theme

Planned Date

Palette

Placement

Design

Detail 1

Detail 2

Notes

Tattoo

Placement

Theme

Planned Date

Palette

Placement

Design

Detail 1

Detail 2

Notes

Tattoo

Placement

Theme

Planned Date

Palette

Placement

Design

Detail 1

Detail 2

Notes

Tattoo

Placement

Theme

Planned Date

Palette

Placement

Design

Detail 1

Detail 2

Notes

Tattoo

Placement

Theme

Planned Date

Palette

Placement

Design

Detail 1

Detail 2

Notes

Tattoo

Placement

Theme

Planned Date

Palette

Placement

Design

Detail 1

Detail 2

Notes

Tattoo

Placement

Theme

Planned Date

Palette

Placement

Design

Detail 1

Detail 2

Notes

Tattoo

Placement

Theme

Planned Date

Palette

Placement

Design

Detail 1

Detail 2

Notes

Tattoo

Placement

Theme

Planned Date

Palette

Placement

Design

Detail 1

Detail 2

Notes

Tattoo

Placement

Theme

Planned Date

Palette

Placement

Design

Detail 1

Detail 2

Notes

Tattoo

Placement

Theme

Planned Date

Palette

Placement

Design

Detail 1

Detail 2

Notes

Tattoo

Placement

Theme

Planned Date

Palette

Placement

Design

Detail 1

Detail 2

Notes

Tattoo

Placement

Theme

Planned Date

Palette

Placement

Design

Detail 1

Detail 2

Notes

Tattoo

Placement

Theme

Planned Date

Palette

Placement

Design

Detail 1

Detail 2

Notes

Tattoo

Placement

Theme

Planned Date

Palette

Placement

Design

Detail 1

Detail 2

Notes

Tattoo

Placement

Theme

Planned Date

Palette

Placement

Design

Detail 1

Detail 2

Notes

Tattoo

Placement

Theme

Planned Date

Palette

Placement

Design

Detail 1

Detail 2

Notes

Tattoo

Placement

Theme

Planned Date

Palette

Placement

Design

Detail 1

Detail 2

Notes

Tattoo

Placement

Theme

Planned Date

Palette

Placement

Design

Detail 1

Detail 2

Notes

Tattoo

Placement

Theme

Planned Date

Palette

Placement

Design

Detail 1

Detail 2

Notes

Tattoo

Placement

Theme

Planned Date

Palette

Placement

Design

Detail 1

Detail 2

Notes

Tattoo

Placement

Theme

Planned Date

Palette

Placement

Design

Detail 1

Detail 2

Notes

Tattoo

Placement

Theme

Planned Date

Palette

Placement

Design

Detail 1

Detail 2

Notes

Tattoo

Placement

Theme

Planned Date

Palette

Placement

Design

Detail 1

Detail 2

Notes

Tattoo

Placement

Theme

Planned Date

Palette

Placement

Design

Detail 1

Detail 2

Notes

Tattoo

Placement

Theme

Planned Date

Palette

Placement

Design

Detail 1

Detail 2

Notes

Tattoo

Placement

Theme

Planned Date

Palette

Placement

Design

Detail 1

Detail 2

Notes

Tattoo

Placement

Theme

Planned Date

Palette

Placement

Design

Detail 1

Detail 2

Notes

Tattoo

Placement

Theme

Planned Date

Palette

Placement

Design

Detail 1

Detail 2

Notes

Tattoo

Placement

Theme

Planned Date

Palette

Placement

Design

Detail 1

Detail 2

Notes

Tattoo

Placement

Theme

Planned Date

Palette

Placement

Design

Detail 1

Detail 2

Notes

Tattoo

Placement

Theme

Planned Date

Palette

Placement

Design

Detail 1

Detail 2

Notes

Tattoo

Placement

Theme

Planned Date

Palette

Placement

Design

Detail 1

Detail 2

Notes

Tattoo

Placement

Theme

Planned Date

Palette

Placement

Design

Detail 1

Detail 2

Notes

Tattoo

Placement

Theme

Planned Date

Palette

Placement

Design

Detail 1

Detail 2

Notes

Tattoo

Placement

Theme

Planned Date

Palette

Placement

Design

Detail 1

Detail 2

Notes

Tattoo

Placement

Theme

Planned Date

Palette

Placement

Design

Detail 1

Detail 2

Notes

Tattoo

Placement

Theme

Planned Date

Palette

Placement

Design

Detail 1

Detail 2

Notes

Tattoo

Placement

Theme

Planned Date

Palette

Placement

Design

Detail 1

Detail 2

Notes

Tattoo

Placement

Theme

Planned Date

Palette

Placement

Design

Detail 1

Detail 2

Notes

Tattoo

Placement

Theme

Planned Date

Palette

Placement

Design

Detail 1

Detail 2

Notes

Tattoo

Placement

Theme

Planned Date

Palette

Placement

Design

Detail 1

Detail 2

Notes

Tattoo

Placement

Theme

Planned Date

Palette

Placement

Design

Detail 1

Detail 2

Notes

Tattoo

Placement

Theme

Planned Date

Palette

Placement

Design

Detail 1

Detail 2

Notes

Tattoo

Placement

Theme

Planned Date

Palette

Placement

Design

Detail 1

Detail 2

Notes

Tattoo

Placement

Theme

Planned Date

Palette

Placement

Design

Detail 1

Detail 2

Notes

Tattoo

Placement

Theme

Planned Date

Palette

Placement

Design

Detail 1

Detail 2

Notes

Tattoo

Placement

Theme

Planned Date

Palette

Placement

Design

Detail 1

Detail 2

Notes

Tattoo

Placement

Theme

Planned Date

Palette

Placement

Design

Detail 1

Detail 2

Notes

Tattoo

Placement

Theme

Planned Date

Palette

Placement

Design

Detail 1

Detail 2

Notes

Tattoo

Placement

Theme

Planned Date

Palette

Placement

Design

Detail 1

Detail 2

Notes

Tattoo

Placement

Theme

Planned Date

Palette

Placement

Design

Detail 1

Detail 2

Notes

Tattoo

Placement

Theme

Planned Date

Palette

Placement

Design

Detail 1

Detail 2

Notes

Tattoo

Placement

Theme

Planned Date

Palette

Placement

Design

Detail 1

Detail 2

Notes

Tattoo

Placement

Theme

Planned Date

Palette

Placement

Design

Detail 1

Detail 2

Notes

Tattoo

Placement

Theme

Planned Date

Palette

Placement

Design

Detail 1

Detail 2

Notes

Tattoo

Placement

Theme

Planned Date

Palette

Placement

Design

Detail 1

Detail 2

Notes

Tattoo

Placement

Theme

Planned Date

Palette

Placement

Design

Detail 1

Detail 2

Notes

Tattoo

Placement

Theme

Planned Date

Palette

Placement

Design

Detail 1

Detail 2

Notes

Tattoo

Placement

Theme

Planned Date

Palette

Placement

Design

Detail 1

Detail 2

Notes

Tattoo

Placement

Theme

Planned Date

Palette

Placement

Design

Detail 1

Detail 2

Notes

Tattoo

Placement

Theme

Planned Date

Palette

Placement

Design

Detail 1

Detail 2

Notes

Tattoo

Placement

Theme

Planned Date

Palette

Placement

Design

Detail 1

Detail 2

Notes

Tattoo

Placement

Theme

Planned Date

Palette

Placement

Design

Detail 1

Detail 2

Notes

Tattoo

Placement

Theme

Planned Date

Palette

Placement

Design

Detail 1

Detail 2

Notes

Tattoo

Placement

Theme

Planned Date

Palette

Placement

Design

Detail 1

Detail 2

Notes

Tattoo

Placement

Theme

Planned Date

Palette

Placement

Design

Detail 1

Detail 2

Notes

Tattoo

Placement

Theme

Planned Date

Palette

Placement

Design

Detail 1

Detail 2

Notes

Tattoo

Placement

Theme

Planned Date

Palette

Placement

Design

Detail 1

Detail 2

Notes

Tattoo

Placement

Theme

Planned Date

Placement

Palette

Design

Detail 1

Detail 2

Notes

Tattoo

Placement

Theme

Planned Date

Palette

Placement

Design

Detail 1

Detail 2

Notes

Tattoo

Placement

Theme

Planned Date

Placement

Palette

Design

Detail 1

Detail 2

Notes

Tattoo

Placement

Theme

Planned Date

Palette

Placement

Design

Detail 1

Detail 2

Notes

Tattoo

Placement

Theme

Planned Date

Palette

Placement

Design

Detail 1

Detail 2

Notes

Tattoo

Placement

Theme

Planned Date

Palette

Placement

Design

Detail 1

Detail 2

Notes

Tattoo

Placement

Theme

Planned Date

Palette

Placement

Design

Detail 1

Detail 2

Notes

Tattoo

Placement

Theme

Planned Date

Palette

Placement

Design

Detail 1

Detail 2

Notes

Tattoo

Placement

Theme

Planned Date

Palette

Placement

Design

Detail 1

Detail 2

Notes

Tattoo

Placement

Theme

Planned Date

Palette

Placement

Design

Detail 1

Detail 2

Notes

Tattoo

Placement

Theme

Planned Date

Palette

Placement

Design

Detail 1

Detail 2

Notes

Tattoo

Placement

Theme

Planned Date

Palette

Placement

Design

Detail 1

Detail 2

Notes

Tattoo

Placement

Theme

Planned Date

Palette

Placement

Design

Detail 1

Detail 2

Notes

Tattoo

Placement

Theme

Planned Date

Palette

Placement

Design

Detail 1

Detail 2

Notes

Tattoo

Placement

Theme

Planned Date

Palette

Placement

Design

Detail 1

Detail 2

Notes

Tattoo

Placement

Theme

Planned Date

Palette

Placement

Design

Detail 1

Detail 2

Notes

Tattoo

Placement

Theme

Planned Date

Palette

Placement

Design

Detail 1

Detail 2

Notes

Tattoo

Placement

Theme

Planned Date

Palette

Placement

Design

Detail 1

Detail 2

Notes

Tattoo

Placement

Theme

Planned Date

Palette

Placement

Design

Detail 1

Detail 2

Notes

Tattoo

Placement

Theme

Planned Date

Palette

Placement

Design

Detail 1

Detail 2

Notes

Tattoo

Placement

Theme

Planned Date

Palette

Placement

Design

Detail 1

Detail 2

Notes

Tattoo

Placement

Theme

Planned Date

Palette

Placement

Design

Detail 1

Detail 2

Notes

Tattoo

Placement

Theme

Planned Date

Palette

Placement

Design

Detail 1

Detail 2

Notes

Tattoo

Placement

Theme

Planned Date

Palette

Placement

Design

Detail 1

Detail 2

Notes

Tattoo

Placement

Theme

Planned Date

Palette

Placement

Design

Detail 1

Detail 2

Notes

Tattoo

Placement

Theme

Planned Date

Palette

Placement

Design

Detail 1

Detail 2

Notes

Tattoo

Placement

Theme

Planned Date

Placement

Palette

Design

Detail 1

Detail 2

Notes

Tattoo

Placement

Theme

Planned Date

Palette

Placement

Design

Detail 1

Detail 2

Notes

Tattoo

Placement

Theme

Planned Date

Palette

Placement

Design

Detail 1

Detail 2

Notes

Tattoo

Placement

Theme

Planned Date

Palette

Placement

Design

Detail 1

Detail 2

Notes

Tattoo

Placement

Theme

Planned Date

Placement

Palette

Design

Detail 1

Detail 2

Notes

Tattoo

Placement

Theme

Planned Date

Palette

Placement

Design

Detail 1

Detail 2

Notes

Tattoo

Placement

Theme

Planned Date

Palette

Placement

Design

Detail 1

Detail 2

Notes

Tattoo

Placement

Theme

Planned Date

Palette

Placement

Design

Detail 1

Detail 2

Notes

Tattoo

Placement

Theme

Planned Date

Palette

Placement

Design

Detail 1

Detail 2

Notes

Tattoo

Placement

Theme

Planned Date

Palette

Placement

Design

Detail 1

Detail 2

Notes

Tattoo

Placement

Theme

Planned Date

Palette

Placement

Design

Detail 1

Detail 2

Notes

Tattoo

Placement

Theme

Planned Date

Palette

Placement

Design

Detail 1

Detail 2

Notes

Tattoo

Placement

Theme

Planned Date

Palette

Placement

Design

Detail 1

Detail 2

Notes

Tattoo

Placement

Theme

Planned Date

Palette

Placement

Design

Detail 1

Detail 2

Notes

Tattoo

Placement

Theme

Planned Date

Palette

Placement

Design

Detail 1

Detail 2

Notes

Tattoo

Placement

Theme

Planned Date

Palette

Placement

Design

Detail 1

Detail 2

Notes

Tattoo

Placement

Theme

Planned Date

Palette

Placement

Design

Detail 1

Detail 2

Notes

Tattoo

Placement

Theme

Planned Date

Palette

Placement

Design

Detail 1

Detail 2

Notes

Tattoo

Placement

Theme

Planned Date

Palette

Placement

Design

Detail 1

Detail 2

Notes

Tattoo

Placement

Theme

Planned Date

Palette

Placement

Design

Detail 1

Detail 2

Notes

Tattoo

Placement

Theme

Planned Date

Palette

Placement

Design

Detail 1

Detail 2

Notes

Tattoo

Placement

Theme

Planned Date

Palette

Placement

Design

Detail 1

Detail 2

Notes

Tattoo

Placement

Theme

Planned Date

Palette

Placement

Design

Detail 1

Detail 2

Notes

Tattoo

Placement

Theme

Planned Date

Palette

Placement

Design

Detail 1

Detail 2

Notes

Tattoo

Placement

Theme

Planned Date

Palette

Placement

Design

Detail 1

Detail 2

Notes

Tattoo

Placement

Theme

Planned Date

Palette

Placement

Design

Detail 1

Detail 2

Notes

Tattoo

Placement

Theme

Planned Date

Palette

Placement

Design

Detail 1

Detail 2

Notes

Tattoo

Placement

Theme

Planned Date

Palette

Placement

Design

Detail 1

Detail 2

Notes

Tattoo

Placement

Theme

Planned Date

Palette

Placement

Design

Detail 1

Detail 2

Notes

Tattoo

Placement

Theme

Planned Date

Palette

Placement

Design

Detail 1

Detail 2

Notes

Tattoo

Placement

Theme

Planned Date

Palette

Placement

Design

Detail 1

Detail 2

Notes

Tattoo

Placement

Theme

Planned Date

Palette

Placement

Design

Detail 1

Detail 2

Notes

Tattoo

Placement

Theme

Planned Date

Palette

Placement

Design

Detail 1

Detail 2

Notes

Tattoo

Placement

Theme

Planned Date

Palette

Placement

Design

Detail 1

Detail 2

Notes

Tattoo

Placement

Theme

Planned Date

Palette

Placement

Design

Detail 1

Detail 2

Notes

Tattoo

Placement

Theme

Planned Date

Palette

Placement

Design

Detail 1

Detail 2

Notes

Tattoo

Placement

Theme

Planned Date

Palette

Placement

Design

Detail 1

Detail 2

Notes

Tattoo

Placement

Theme

Planned Date

Palette

Placement

Design

Detail 1

Detail 2

Notes

Tattoo

Placement

Theme

Planned Date

Palette

Placement

Design

Detail 1

Detail 2

Notes

Tattoo

Placement

Theme

Planned Date

Palette

Placement

Design

Detail 1

Detail 2

Notes

Tattoo

Placement

Theme

Planned Date

Placement

Palette

Design

Detail 1

Detail 2

Notes

Tattoo

Placement

Theme

Planned Date

Palette

Placement

Design

Detail 1

Detail 2

Notes

Tattoo

Placement

Theme

Planned Date

Palette

Placement

Design

Detail 1

Detail 2

Notes

Tattoo

Placement

Theme

Planned Date

Palette

Placement

Design

Detail 1

Detail 2

Notes

Tattoo

Placement

Theme

Planned Date

Palette

Placement

Design

Detail 1

Detail 2

Notes

Tattoo

Placement

Theme

Planned Date

Palette

Placement

Design

Detail 1

Detail 2

Notes

Tattoo

Placement

Theme

Planned Date

Palette

Placement

Design

Detail 1

Detail 2

Notes

Tattoo

Placement

Theme

Planned Date

Palette

Placement

Design

Detail 1

Detail 2

Notes

Tattoo

Placement

Theme

Planned Date

Palette

Placement

Design

Detail 1

Detail 2

Notes

Tattoo

Placement

Theme

Planned Date

Palette

Placement

Design

Detail 1

Detail 2

Notes

Tattoo

Placement

Theme

Planned Date

Palette

Placement

Design

Detail 1

Detail 2

Notes

Tattoo

Placement

Theme

Planned Date

Palette

Placement

Design

Detail 1

Detail 2

Notes

Tattoo

Placement

Theme

Planned Date

Palette

Placement

Design

Detail 1

Detail 2

Notes

Tattoo

Placement

Theme

Planned Date

Palette

Placement

Design

Detail 1

Detail 2

Notes

Tattoo

Placement

Theme

Planned Date

Palette

Placement

Design

Detail 1

Detail 2

Notes

Tattoo

Placement

Theme

Planned Date

Palette

Placement

Design

Detail 1

Detail 2

Notes

Tattoo

Placement

Theme

Planned Date

Palette

Placement

Design

Detail 1

Detail 2

Notes

Tattoo

Placement

Theme

Planned Date

Palette

Placement

Design

Detail 1

Detail 2

Notes

Tattoo

Placement

Theme

Planned Date

Palette

Placement

Design

Detail 1

Detail 2

Notes

Tattoo

Placement

Theme

Planned Date

Palette

Placement

Design

Detail 1

Detail 2

Notes

Tattoo

Placement

Theme

Planned Date

Palette

Placement

Design

Detail 1

Detail 2

Notes

Tattoo

Placement

Theme

Planned Date

Palette

Placement

Design

Detail 1

Detail 2

Notes

Tattoo

Placement

Theme

Planned Date

Palette

Placement

Design

Detail 1

Detail 2

Notes

Tattoo

Placement

Theme

Planned Date

Palette

Placement

Design

Detail 1

Detail 2

Notes

Tattoo

Placement

Theme

Planned Date

Palette

Placement

Design

Detail 1

Detail 2

Notes

Tattoo

Placement

Theme

Planned Date

Palette

Placement

Design

Detail 1

Detail 2

Notes

Tattoo

Placement

Theme

Planned Date

Palette

Placement

Design

Detail 1

Detail 2

Notes

Tattoo

Placement

Theme

Planned Date

Palette

Placement

Design

Detail 1

Detail 2

Notes

Tattoo

Placement

Theme

Planned Date

Placement

Palette

Design

Detail 1

Detail 2

Notes

Tattoo

Placement

Theme

Planned Date

Palette

Placement

Design

Detail 1

Detail 2

Notes

Tattoo

Placement

Theme

Planned Date

Palette

Placement

Design

Detail 1

Detail 2

Notes

Tattoo

Placement

Theme

Planned Date

Palette

Placement

Design

Detail 1

Detail 2

Notes

Tattoo

Placement

Theme

Planned Date

Palette

Placement

Design

Detail 1

Detail 2

Notes

Tattoo

Placement

Theme

Planned Date

Palette

Placement

Design

Detail 1

Detail 2

Notes

Tattoo

Placement

Theme

Planned Date

Palette

Placement

Design

Detail 1

Detail 2

Notes

Tattoo

Placement

Theme

Planned Date

Palette

Placement

Design

Detail 1

Detail 2

Notes

Tattoo

Placement

Theme

Planned Date

Palette

Placement

Design

Detail 1

Detail 2

Notes

Tattoo

Placement

Theme

Planned Date

Palette

Placement

Design

Detail 1

Detail 2

Notes

Tattoo

Placement

Theme

Planned Date

Palette

Placement

Design

Detail 1

Detail 2

Notes

Tattoo

Placement

Theme

Planned Date

Palette

Placement

Design

Detail 1

Detail 2

Notes

Tattoo

Placement

Theme

Planned Date

Palette

Placement

Design

Detail 1

Detail 2

Notes

www.ingramcontent.com/pod-product-compliance
Lightning Source LLC
LaVergne TN
LVHW060140080526
838202LV00049B/4033